NEW ZEALAND

By Charis Mather

BookLife PUBLISHING

©2022
BookLife Publishing Ltd.
King's Lynn, Norfolk
PE30 4LS, UK

All rights reserved.
Printed in Poland.

A catalogue record for this book is available from the British Library.

ISBN: 978-1-80155-589-0

Written by:
Charis Mather

Edited by:
William Anthony

Designed by:
Gareth Liddington

All facts, statistics, web addresses and URLs in this book were verified as valid and accurate at time of writing. No responsibility for any changes to external websites or references can be accepted by either the author or publisher.

WEST NORTHAMPTONSHIRE COUNCIL	
60000532008	
Askews & Holts	
BB	

Image Credits

All images are courtesy of Shutterstock.com, unless otherwise specified. With thanks to Getty Images, Thinkstock Photo and iStockphoto.

Cover – Umomos, Blue Planet Studio. 2–3 – Rudy Balasko. 4–5 – Shanti Hesse, Matis75. 6–7 – GocmenStudio, Stefan Mokrzecki. 8–9 – ChameleonsEye, lukefranklinimages. 10–11 – Prachaya Roekdeethaweesab, Christian Heinegg, Crown Studios Ltd. 12–13 – aaron choi, Jumussoi94. 14–15 – Gr8, Vadim Boussenko. 16–17 – mushtaq saad, Michal Tesar. 18–19 ChameleonsEye, Paolo Bona. 20–21 – Caroline Ryan, Vee Snijders. 22–23 travellight, criskorah.

CONTENTS

Page 4   Country to Country
Page 6   Today's Trip Is to... New Zealand!
Page 8   Auckland
Page 10   Famous New Zealanders
Page 12   Aoraki
Page 14   Volcanoes
Page 16   Matariki
Page 18   Haka
Page 20   Animals
Page 22   Before You Go...
Page 24   Glossary and Index

Words that look like this can be found in the glossary on page 24.

COUNTRY TO COUNTRY

What country do you live in?

A country is an area of land that usually has clear **borders** which can be seen on a map. Countries usually have different ways of living and different rules for the people that live there.

There are many countries in the world. We can find amazing things in each one. What country do you think we are going to visit today?

Do you know anyone who lives in a different country to you?

TODAY'S TRIP IS TO...
NEW ZEALAND!

New Zealand

New Zealand is made up of two large **islands**, called North Island and South Island. There are also many smaller islands that are part of New Zealand. Can you see New Zealand on the map?

FACT FILE

Capital city: Wellington
Main language: English
Currency: New Zealand dollar
Flag:

Currency is the type of money that is used by a country.

AUCKLAND

We are in Auckland, where the Sky Tower is. The Sky Tower is the tallest building in the **Southern Hemisphere**. It is over 320 metres tall and has a great view at the top.

The Sky Tower has a famous turning restaurant.

Auckland also has a famous hill called Maungakiekie. New Zealand's **Indigenous** Māori people built a village at the top of this hill. You can still see parts of it today.

Maungakiekie is also called One Tree Hill. Can you guess why?

FAMOUS NEW ZEALANDERS

Kate Sheppard (1847–1934)

What famous New Zealanders do you know?

Kate Sheppard helped women get the same **rights** as men. Before Kate, women were not allowed to make big decisions or do the same things as men.

Whina Cooper was a Māori leader who helped when Māori land was being taken from them.

Whina Cooper (1895–1994)

Edmund Hillary was an explorer who climbed Mount Everest with Tibetan guide Tenzing Norgay. They were the first to get to the top.

Edmund Hillary (1919–2008)

AORAKI

Aoraki is not as high as Mount Everest, but it is the highest mountain in New Zealand. The top of Aoraki is over 3,000 metres high and is often visited by climbers.

Aoraki is also called Mount Cook.

If you visit Aoraki, you might get to see one of New Zealand's kea parrots. Kea parrots live near mountains. You can also see icy **glaciers** and clear views of the night stars.

Kea bird

VOLCANOES

New Zealand has a lot of **volcanoes**. The island of Rangitoto is one of New Zealand's many volcanoes.

Rangitoto first appeared around 600 years ago.

Mount Rangitoto is home to the world's largest Pōhutukawa forest. Pōhutukawa trees have bright-red flowers. These trees are an important part of Indigenous Māori stories.

Pōhutukawa trees are also called New Zealand Christmas trees.

MATARIKI

Māori people celebrate Matariki when these stars appear.

Many Māori people celebrate the new year around the middle of winter. Lots of people who are not Māori also join in. This festival is called Matariki, which is the Māori name for a group of stars.

During Matariki, people remember their loved ones and plan for the year ahead. They also celebrate the people and **culture** of New Zealand. Families have events that include art, dancing and **Haka** performances.

Fireworks are sometimes used to celebrate Matariki.

HAKA

Māori people perform the Haka in a group.

The Haka dance is important in Māori culture. Haka performers stamp their feet, slap their bodies, pull faces and chant together. It is a show of pride.

In the past, this dance was used by Māori fighters or when groups would meet together. Now it can be seen at special events such as weddings and sports games.

The New Zealand All Blacks rugby team often performs the Haka.

ANIMALS

New Zealand is also known for having lots and lots of sheep. The number of sheep is now going down, but New Zealand still sells lots of lamb and wool.

New Zealand used to have about 70 million sheep.

Can you think of any birds that cannot fly?

The kiwi bird is an animal that can only be found in New Zealand. The kiwi has long, thin feathers and strong legs, but it cannot fly!

BEFORE YOU GO...

If you ever visit New Zealand, make sure to see Piopiotahi and the Waitomo Caves. Piopiotahi is a beautiful area known for its black **coral**.

Piopiotahi is also called Milford Sound.

The Waitomo Caves are home to thousands of glow-worms. They might look like little lights, but they are actually alive. Glow-worms light up the rocks and reflect in the water.

What have you learnt about New Zealand today?

GLOSSARY

borders	lines that show where one place ends and another begins
coral	a hard material formed on the bottom of the sea by the skeletons of small animals
culture	the traditions, ideas and ways of life of a group of people
glaciers	large areas of ice that move very slowly
Haka	a type of Maori dance used in special events, often performed with chanting and powerful movements
Indigenous	to do with the first people to live somewhere
islands	areas of land that are surrounded by water
rights	the options people have about what they can have and do
Southern Hemisphere	the lower half of the Earth
volcanoes	mountains that can be formed with hot gases and melted rock, which is called lava

INDEX

birds 13, 21
caves 22–23
dances 18–19
islands 6, 14
Māori 9, 11, 15–16, 18–19
mountains 12–13
stars 13, 16
trees 9, 15